THE
HUMAN PATH
ACROSS THE CONTINENTS

PATHWAYS THROUGH
EUROPE

John C. Miles

CRABTREE
PUBLISHING COMPANY
WWW.CRABTREEBOOKS.COM

CRABTREE
PUBLISHING COMPANY
WWW.CRABTREEBOOKS.COM

Author: John C. Miles

Editorial director: Kathy Middleton

Editors: Rachel Cooke, Janine Deschenes

Design: Jeni Child

Photo research:
   FFP Consulting; Tammy McGarr

Proofreader: Melissa Boyce

Print and production coordinator:
   Katherine Berti

Produced for Crabtree Publishing Company by
FFP Consulting Limited

Images
t=Top, b=Bottom, tl=Top Left, tr=Top Right, bl=Bottom Left,
br=Bottom Right, c=Center, lc=Left Center, rc=Right Center

Alamy
   Martin Bond: p. 7t; Novarc Images: p. 15t; Christoph Rueegg: p. 19t

Shutterstock
   Alexandros Michailidis: p. 5b; Oliverouge 3: p. 6–7b;
   imagestockdesign: p. 9rc; Dave Porter: p. 10–11b; northallertonman:
   p. 11tr; lou armor: p. 11lc; Suwipat Lorsiripaiboon: p. 13t;
   Cinematographer: p. 15r; spatuletail: p. 21rc; Christian Mueller:
   p. 21b; Tupungato: p. 23lc; Marek Poplawski: p. 24–25b; MevZup:
   p. 25t; marekusz: p. 27t; Semmick Photo: p. 27c; Jordan Tan: p. 28b;
   Jaroslaw Kilian: p. 29c

All other images from Shutterstock

Maps: Jeni Child

Library and Archives Canada Cataloguing in Publication

Title: Pathways through Europe / John C. Miles.
Names: Miles, John C., 1960- author.
Description: Series statement: The human path across the continents |
   Includes index.
Identifiers: Canadiana (print) 20190112085 | Canadiana (ebook) 20190112093
   ISBN 9780778766353 (hardcover) |
   ISBN 9780778766483 (softcover) |
   ISBN 9781427124005 (HTML)
Subjects: LCSH: Human ecology—Europe—Juvenile literature. |
   LCSH: Europe—Juvenile literature.
Classification: LCC GF540 .M55 2019 | DDC j304.2094—dc23

Library of Congress Cataloging-in-Publication Data

Names: Miles, John C. (John Christian), 1960- author.
Title: Pathways through Europe / John C. Miles.
Description: New York : Crabtree Publishing Company, 2019. |
   Series: The human path across the continents | Includes index.
Identifiers: LCCN 2019023326 (print) | LCCN 2019023327 (ebook)
   ISBN 9780778766353 (hardcover) |
   ISBN 9780778766483 (paperback) |
   ISBN 9781427124005 (ebook)
Subjects: LCSH: Human ecology--Europe--Juvenile literature. |
   Nature--Effect of human beings on--Europe--Juvenile literature. |
   Physical geography--Europe--Juvenile literature. |
   Europe--Environmental conditions--Juvenile literature.
Classification: LCC GF540 .M55 2019 (print) | LCC GF540 (ebook) |
   DDC 304.2094--dc23
LC record available at https://lccn.loc.gov/2019023326
LC ebook record available at https://lccn.loc.gov/2019023327

Crabtree Publishing Company
www.crabtreebooks.com   1-800-387-7650

Printed in the U.S.A./082019/CG20190712

Published in Canada
Crabtree Publishing
616 Welland Ave.
St. Catharines, Ontario
L2M 5V6

Published in the United States
Crabtree Publishing
PMB 59051
350 Fifth Avenue, 59th Floor
New York, New York 10118

Published in the United Kingdom
Crabtree Publishing
Maritime House
Basin Road North, Hove
BN41 1WR

Published in Australia
Crabtree Publishing
Unit 3–5 Currumbin Court
Capalaba
QLD 4157

CONTENTS

EUROPE

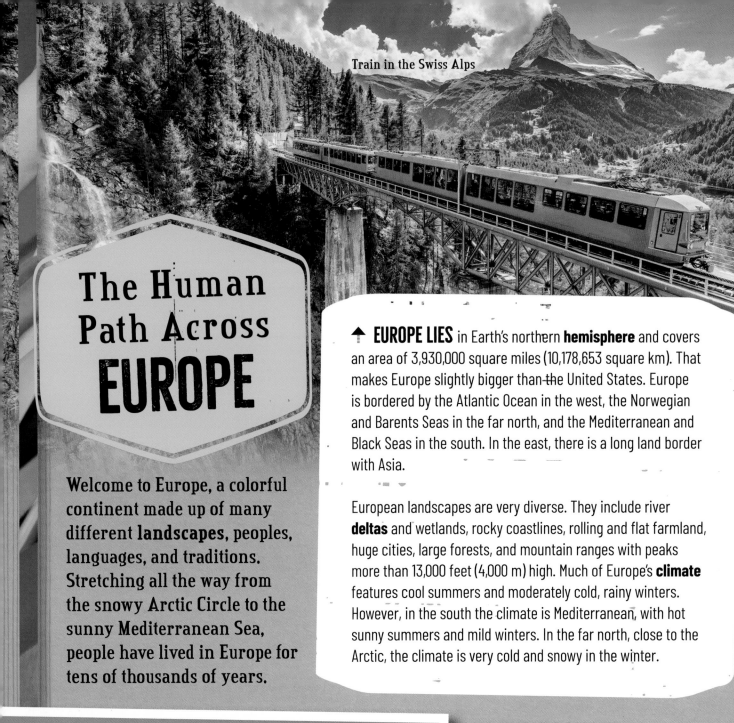

Train in the Swiss Alps

The Human Path Across EUROPE

Welcome to Europe, a colorful continent made up of many different **landscapes**, peoples, languages, and traditions. Stretching all the way from the snowy Arctic Circle to the sunny Mediterranean Sea, people have lived in Europe for tens of thousands of years.

⬆ **EUROPE LIES** in Earth's northern **hemisphere** and covers an area of 3,930,000 square miles (10,178,653 square km). That makes Europe slightly bigger than the United States. Europe is bordered by the Atlantic Ocean in the west, the Norwegian and Barents Seas in the far north, and the Mediterranean and Black Seas in the south. In the east, there is a long land border with Asia.

European landscapes are very diverse. They include river **deltas** and wetlands, rocky coastlines, rolling and flat farmland, huge cities, large forests, and mountain ranges with peaks more than 13,000 feet (4,000 m) high. Much of Europe's **climate** features cool summers and moderately cold, rainy winters. However, in the south the climate is Mediterranean, with hot sunny summers and mild winters. In the far north, close to the Arctic, the climate is very cold and snowy in the winter.

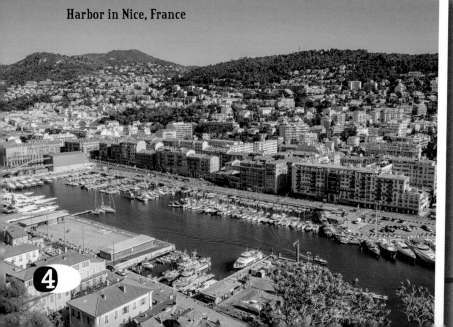

Harbor in Nice, France

◀ **EUROPE'S COASTAL SETTLEMENTS** have always been important, developing around natural harbors such as Nice, in France. Over the centuries, many Europeans have depended on ships and the sea for their living. In addition, major rivers, such as the Rhine and the Danube, flow through many countries. These rivers have acted as transportation superhighways for hundreds of years, helping towns and cities to develop beside them.

ICELAND

Two thousand years ago, most of Europe was ruled by the **Roman Empire**. After the empire collapsed, many small kingdoms and states came into being. They often went to war with each other. However, over time, many united to form countries such as the **United Kingdom**, France, Germany, Spain, and Italy.

Norwegian Sea

FINLAND

RUSSIA

NORWAY

SWEDEN

ESTONIA

LATVIA

North Sea

Baltic Sea

LITHUANIA

DENMARK

RUSSIA

IRELAND

BELARUS

UNITED KINGDOM

NETHERLANDS

POLAND

GERMANY

UKRAINE

BELGIUM

LUXEMBOURG

CZECH REPUBLIC

SLOVAKIA

MOLDOVA

Atlantic Ocean

LIECHTENSTEIN

AUSTRIA

HUNGARY

ROMANIA

FRANCE

SWITZERLAND

SLOVENIA

CROATIA

Black Sea

ANDORRA

SAN MARINO

BOSNIA AND HERZEGOVINA

SERBIA

BULGARIA

MONACO

KOSOVO

PORTUGAL

ITALY

MONTENEGRO

NORTH MACEDONIA

TURKEY

SPAIN

VATICAN CITY

ALBANIA

Mediterranean Sea

GREECE

CYPRUS

MALTA

Barents Sea

EU building, Brussels, Belgium

◀ **AFTER TWO DISASTROUS** world wars in the twentieth century, Europe's leaders formed the European Union (EU). Eventually this united 28 countries. They agreed to allow people and goods to move freely across borders. Today, the EU has a population of around 513 million, and is a major world **economy**.

This book examines the physical and human geography of Europe through a series of journeys. Some of these journeys are long, and cross several country borders. Others are shorter, and show how diverse Europe's geography can be, even within a small area.

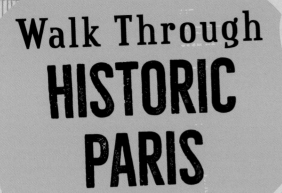

Walk Through
HISTORIC
PARIS

In 1993, the city of Paris, France, opened an unusual park named the Promenade Plantée. This park is a raised walkway. It was created from a 2.9-mile (4.7 km) section of railroad that closed in 1969. Today, both residents and tourists walk and cycle among its trees, enjoying green space in the middle of the city.

▶ **THE BASTILLE AREA,** on the east side of the city center, is the starting point for our walk. This is where Paris's modern **opera** house, the Opéra Bastille, is located. There is also a monument to the Bastille prison, where, for centuries, political prisoners were locked up.

PARIS

Opéra Bastille

Boulevard Périphérique

SEINE RIVER

Jardin de Reuilly

Bois de Vincennes

Promenade Plantée walk

PARIS

Bastille monument and opera house

People enjoying the Promenade Plantée

Thierry and Marg are street entertainers who perform at several locations in and around central Paris. The two are often found near the Promenade Plantée on summer weekends. They might make enough money from locals and tourists to pay a part of their rent.

⬆ **THE PROMENADE PLANTÉE** begins as a raised path lined with trees and flower beds, snaking through the 12th district of Paris. Underneath is the Viaduc des Arts, which is home to craft workshops and stores. Staircases and elevators connect the upper and lower levels.

After passing over the Jardin de Reuilly park on a footbridge, the Promenade Plantée splits into two lanes. One is for **pedestrians**, the other is for cyclists and in-line skaters. Further on, the tree-lined route passes through tunnels. Hundreds of bats make their homes in the tunnel walls. You can walk all the way from the center of Paris to the Boulevard Périphérique. This busy highway forms a ring around central Paris. On the other side of the highway is the Bois de Vincennes, the city's largest park.

⬇ **RICH AND POOR** neighborhoods exist side by side in Paris, as in many European cities. From the raised sections of the Promenade Plantée you can see fine old buildings containing apartments belonging to the wealthy. In contrast, you can also spot **social housing** where less well-off people live. One of the aims of opening the Promenade Plantée was to give local people regular access to some green space. This is part of a process of renewing areas formerly used for the **manufacturing industry.** Now parks and housing replace old factories. The same happens in many other European cities.

➤ Apartment buildings in Paris

Make a Pilgrimage Through SPAIN

ATLANTIC OCEAN

SPAIN

Santiago de Compostela

León

Burgos

PORTUGAL

↓ Cathedral at Santiago de Compostela

SPAIN

Hundreds of years ago, in **medieval** times, **Christians** made long, difficult journeys to visit the burial places of important **saints**. These journeys were known as **pilgrimages**. Many pilgrimage routes are still in use today. People who walk them may do so because of their religious beliefs, or to enjoy an active vacation.

↑ **SANTIAGO DE COMPOSTELA,** in northwestern Spain, is one of Europe's most important pilgrimage sites. Its cathedral is thought to be the burial place of Saint James, a close follower of Jesus. **Pilgrims** walked to Santiago, believing that by doing so they would gain favor with God. As more visitors traveled there, a city grew up around the cathedral. Today, nearly 100,000 people live there. Many of them still rely on the business brought to the city by pilgrims and tourists.

FRANCE

Saint-Jean-Pied-de-Port

Pamplona

PYRENEES MOUNTAINS

Camino Francés
pilgrimage route

PAMPLONA is the first major Spanish city pilgrims enter after crossing the Pyrenees Mountains. It is famous for the "running of the bulls" in July, an event still popular in Spain though criticized for its treatment of animals. Pamploma is the economic center of the region of Navarra. It is home to metalworking and food-processing industries. Its position on the French Way helped it grow to become this important center.

MORE THAN 20 ROUTES lead to Santiago. Towns, churches, and **hostels** were founded along the different routes to help the pilgrims. One of the most popular paths today is the Camino Francés (French Way). This begins in southwestern France, crosses the Spanish border, and runs through northern Spain. More than 300,000 people travel this route every year. Pilgrims can begin the French Way at Saint-Jean-Pied-de-Port. There, they are given a "passport" which is stamped to show that they have completed the various stages of the route. Signs with seashells (the symbol of Saint James) mark the way.

Pilgrims in northern Spain

Bull-running festival, Pamplona

Next, the route enters Castile and León, the largest region in Spain. This area features mountain ranges and high **plateaus**. Pilgrims pass by historic walled cities such as Burgos, famous for its cathedral, and León. From there, they cross into the region of Galicia, which is cooler, wetter, and greener. This is because the climate is influenced by the Atlantic Ocean. Santiago de Compostela is Galicia's capital, and the journey's end for the pilgrims.

PEOPLE ALONG THE WAY

Miguel is 23 years old and studies in Pamplona. He works part time in a restaurant, serving tourists. Miguel often chats to his pilgrim customers who pass through the city throughout the year, and enjoys hearing their stories. He also likes the excitement of the bull-running festival, but prefers his work at quieter times of the year.

Fast Train From LONDON

London and the River Thames

The United Kingdom (UK) is the country in which railroads were invented in the early 1800s. By the 1850s, its capital, London, was linked by train with the Scottish capital of Edinburgh. Today, this busy rail route carries thousands of passengers every day.

↑ **LONDON** is the largest city in both the UK and western Europe, with 8.7 million inhabitants. Thanks to its location on the River Thames, it has been the center of government and an important **port** for nearly 2,000 years. London is also situated at the heart of the UK's railroad, highway, and airport networks. This has helped the city grow into Europe's biggest financial and business center, as people can travel easily to and from London.

You board the train to Edinburgh, named the *Flying Scotsman*, at London's King's Cross Station. First, the train travels through the seemingly endless **suburbs** of London. The city grew outward when rapid trains cut the travel time to the center, allowing city workers to live in nearby towns. Over time, more and more houses were built and the urban area of Greater London grew.

SCOTLAND — rail journey
Firth of Forth
Edinburgh
NORTH SEA
Newcastle
Pennine Hills
North York Moors
York
ENGLAND
WALES
London
River Thames

UNITED KINGDOM

A London-to-Edinburgh train

82204

TWO HOURS NORTH from London, you reach the attractive medieval city of York. It lies in an area of good farming land known as the Vale of York, bordered by the wild North York Moors and the Pennine Hills. Tourism is York's most important industry, bringing in millions of dollars and creating hundreds of jobs. Visitors come to see York's cathedral and the UK's National Railway Museum.

Next stop is Newcastle, where the train crosses the River Tyne. Thanks to the river, the city used to be home to shipbuilding. But industry in the north of England has declined because it is now cheaper to manufacture things in other countries. People now work in digital technology, retail, culture, and tourism.

Historic steam train at York railway station

WE END OUR TRIP IN EDINBURGH, after a distance of 400 miles (644 km). This is Scotland's second-largest city and its capital. About half a million people live there. The city is found on the Firth of Forth, an inlet of the sea, and is built on seven hills shaped by **glaciers** thousands of years ago. As a capital city, it has long been a center for education, law, and medicine. It is also known for its art and theater.

Edinburgh holds arts and theater festivals in August

Pause for REFLECTION

- What factors influence where towns and cities are located?
- Why do you think railroads helped London to grow?
- Imagine a major industry in your town or city closes. What would the consequences be? Now think about alternative industries. Is there any feature in your town that might attract tourists and create new jobs?

Visit Norway's
SAMI LANDS

At the very top of Europe lies the country of Norway. And at the very top of Norway lies Finnmark county. Its very cold climate makes survival there difficult. But for centuries this challenge has been overcome by the Sami people.

↑ **TO REACH FINNMARK,** you take a plane from Oslo, Norway's capital, to Tromso. There, you change to a smaller aircraft for a flight to Alta. As you fly up the Norwegian coastline, you can see many **fjords**, or sea inlets. Small settlements are located on the narrow strips of land beside each fjord. For many people here, fishing is still an important way of life.

Because northern Norway is so close to the **North Pole**, it has nearly 24 hours of darkness in winter. The entire region is covered with snow. In the summer, on the other hand, there are nearly 24 hours of daylight. In this season, the sun never really sets.

Alta
Tromso
Plane flight
SWEDEN
FINLAND
NORWAY
Oslo
RUSSIA

FINNMARK
Alta
Karasjok
Kautokeino

A Sami man with reindeer

Tobejas grew up in a Sami community. After studying business at college, he started a lodge near Karasjok that caters to tourists who want to experience Sami culture. He employs eight people and hopes to expand his business in the future.

↑ THE SAMI are Europe's northernmost people. They have lived in subarctic parts of Norway, Sweden, Finland, and Russia since ancient times. **Herding** reindeer is key to the Sami way of life. The people get meat and clothing from these tough arctic animals. Tourism in Sami lands is also becoming more important.

From Alta, you can travel east by four-wheel-drive vehicle or even snowmobile. In the east, there are large, protected wilderness areas, such as the Stabbursdalen National Park and Paistunturi Wilderness Area. Forests, rivers, and lakes cover the land. Tourists can also travel by cross-country skis or sleds pulled by reindeers.

↓ THE AURORA BOREALIS, or northern lights, is one astonishing feature of the subarctic region. This natural event takes the form of a glow in the night sky, or even shimmering curtains of light. These can be green, red, or other colors. Many people travel to the north of Norway to watch the northern lights.

Many visitors stay in the two main Sami towns, Karasjok and Kautokeino. These small towns have only a few thousand residents, but have developed into centers of Sami culture. The Sami Parliament of Norway and a Sami radio station are in Karasjok. In Kautokeino, 90 percent of the population speak Sami. There is a museum of Sami culture, the Sami University College, and a Sami-language theater.

The aurora borealis

Commute From
SWEDEN TO DENMARK

DENMARK | Oresund Strait | SWEDEN

Copenhagen | Airport | Drogden Tunnel

Peberholm Island | Oresund Bridge | Malmö

For centuries, the Danish capital city of Copenhagen and the Swedish city of Malmö have faced each other across a narrow stretch of water called the Oresund **Strait**. In 2000, a bridge and tunnel crossing opened, linking the two cities. This created new opportunities for the people who live there.

EUROPE

▼ **COPENHAGEN** has a population of nearly 800,000 people. It is the cultural, economic, and governmental center of Denmark. Malmö, 26 miles (42 km) away across the Oresund Strait, is Sweden's third-largest city, with a population of more than 300,000. Malmö developed in the 1800s as a center for shipbuilding and other manufacturing industries. In the late twentieth century, many of these industries closed due to competition from countries in Asia. Many people lost their jobs as a result.

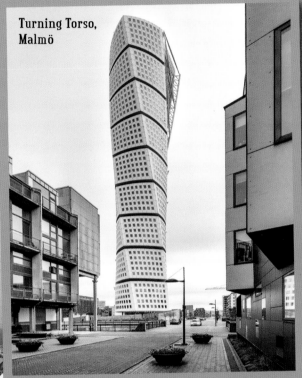

Oresund Bridge and Drogden Tunnel entrance

▶ THE ORESUND BRIDGE

stretches from the Swedish coast to the tiny island of Peberholm, in the middle of the strait. It is the longest combined road and rail bridge in Europe, at 25,738 feet (7,845 m). The Oresund Bridge carries two roadways and two train tracks. Having first traveled over the bridge, **commuters** from Sweden then pass through the 13,287-foot (4,050 m) Drogden Tunnel, arriving in Denmark.

One reason for building a tunnel under the strait was to avoid any risk to aircraft taking off or landing at Copenhagen's airport, which is nearby. Another reason for using a tunnel instead of a bridge was to stop winter ice from building up around the bridge and blocking the busy waterway. The Oresund Strait is a main shipping route to and from the Baltic Sea.

Turning Torso, Malmö

Skyline of Copenhagen, Denmark

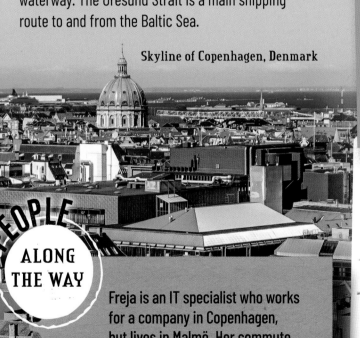

PEOPLE ALONG THE WAY

Freja is an IT specialist who works for a company in Copenhagen, but lives in Malmö. Her commute by train via the Oresund crossing takes her about one hour. She used to live in a cramped apartment in Copenhagen, but since moving to Malmö she can afford a much bigger home.

▲ MAJOR ECONOMIC BENEFITS have

resulted from building the Oresund Bridge. Workers in overcrowded Copenhagen, where housing is expensive, can live in Sweden, where the cost of living is lower. Swedish workers can commute to Denmark, where there are more jobs.

The city of Malmö has also improved, thanks to the bridge. A new university opened and the harbor has been redeveloped with waterside housing. The Turning Torso skyscraper was built in 2005. This building, the tallest in Scandinavia, has 54 stories and contains 147 apartments.

15

Rhine Barge to SWITZERLAND

NORTH SEA
NETHERLANDS
Rotterdam
Rhine Delta
GERMANY
Düsseldorf
Cologne
BELGIUM
Rhine Gorge
Rhine River
LUXEMBOURG
FRANCE
AUSTRIA
Basel
EUROPE
SWITZERLAND
Alps
ITALY

Every day, river barges loaded with **cargo containers** leave the Dutch port of Rotterdam, bound for Switzerland. They make the journey on the 766-mile (1,233 km) long Rhine River, which has been a major European transportation highway for hundreds of years.

▼ **ROTTERDAM,** with a population of more than 600,000, is the second-largest city in the Netherlands. It has become Europe's largest port, thanks to its location on a delta, where the Rhine and two other major rivers empty into the North Sea. Goods from around the world are unloaded from ships there to be transported along the river by barges. Chemicals, food products, cars, oil, gas, and coal are all moved along the waterways.

Barges travel east inland through the flat Dutch landscape. Many parts of the Netherlands lie below sea level. Although the country is protected by walls called **dikes**, it is still at risk of flooding from rising sea levels, due to **climate change**.

Rotterdam, the Netherlands

Barges passing through the Rhine Gorge

Pause for REFLECTION

- Why do you think so many major cities have grown up along the Rhine?
- What effects do you think the development of industry had on the Rhine-Ruhr region?
- Why do you think barges are still used when there are other options available, such as road and air transportation?

Crossing the German border, you travel into the Ruhr region. Many kinds of industries can be found there. The Ruhr developed in the 1800s due to its coal mines. Local cities such as Essen then became centers of iron and steel production. The Rhine-Ruhr region also includes the business city of Düsseldorf, and Cologne, a center for media production.

THE RHINE GORGE comes next. A gorge has towering cliffs on both sides of a river, creating a dramatic landscape. The climate there is suitable for growing grapes. This makes the area important for winemaking. Tourism is also a major industry. Many cruise ships chug along the river. Farther up river, the Rhine forms the boundary between France and Germany.

Basel, Switzerland

BASEL, Switzerland's only water port, is our journey's end. This border city of 180,000 people is also a road, air, and railroad transportation hub. Switzerland is a wealthy country, but expensive to live in. Many people commute each day from nearby France to work in Basel. The Rhine River continues on into the Alps—the mountains where it has its source. But our barge will now load up with new cargo containers, turn around, and take the long journey back downriver to Rotterdam.

Journey Under the ALPS

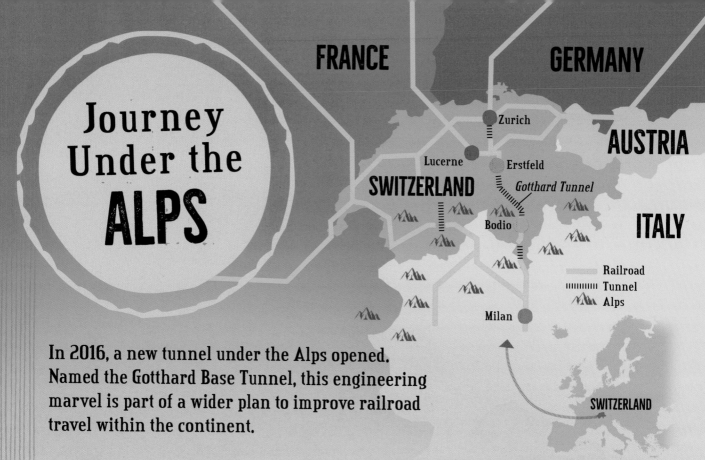

FRANCE

GERMANY

AUSTRIA

ITALY

Zurich

Lucerne

SWITZERLAND

Erstfeld

Gotthard Tunnel

Bodio

Milan

Railroad
Tunnel
Alps

SWITZERLAND

In 2016, a new tunnel under the Alps opened. Named the Gotthard Base Tunnel, this engineering marvel is part of a wider plan to improve railroad travel within the continent.

▼ **THE ALPS** are Europe's largest mountain range. They cover parts of eight countries, including Switzerland, Italy, and Austria. People have lived there since ancient times. They settled in fertile valleys and around the edges of mountain lakes. Traditional activities, such as cattle farming, still operate today. These exist alongside modern tourist industries, such as skiing, that are important to the region's economy.

For thousands of years, Europeans used passes, or natural corridors in the mountains, to cross the Alps. But the passes were very dangerous in winter because they were easily blocked by ice and snow. In 1882, the Saint Gotthard tunnel opened. It connected Lucerne in Switzerland by train with Milan in Italy. Other rail and road tunnels followed, making travel across the Alps safer and quicker.

Cattle in the Alps, Austria

A train comes out of the Gotthard Base Tunnel

Pause for
REFLECTION

- Do you think the environmental benefits of projects such as the Gotthard Base Tunnel are worth the enormous cost of building them?
- What are the advantages of railroads over road or air transportation?

Milan, Italy, with the Alps behind

↑ THE NEW GOTTHARD TUNNEL is

more than 35 miles (57 km) long, making it the world's longest and deepest railroad tunnel. It is so long that the weather is different at either end. For example, at Erstfeld, the northern entrance, winters are cold and snowy, typical of an alpine climate. Bodio, the southern entrance, is warmer and sunnier, as it is closer to Italy and its Mediterranean climate.

The tunnel took 17 years to build and cost billions of dollars. It has helped improve train speeds and cargo transportation between northern and southern Europe. By moving goods on trains through the tunnel, many trucks have been taken off the roads. This reduces air pollution and noise. It is also hoped more people will travel by train instead of by car or airplane. This too helps keep the air clean.

↑ MILAN, Italy's business and fashion center, is the starting point for high-speed passenger trains under the Alps. After passing through the Gotthard Base Tunnel at speeds of up to 155 miles per hour (250 kph), trains enter central Switzerland. After a journey of about three and a half hours, passengers arrive in Zurich. Home to many banks, this wealthy city is the financial capital of Switzerland. Both major cities welcome the new fast link of the Gotthard Base Tunnel between them.

By Water Bus Through VENICE

At the top of the Adriatic Sea in Italy is a shallow **lagoon** filled with islands. The unique city of Venice is found there. Surrounded by water and built on several islands, Venice is famous for its boats and **canals**.

⬆ **VENICE** is a city built on water. Originally, people from the mainland moved to the lagoon to find safety from wars. They built houses by hammering wooden posts into the soft mud to create **foundations**. Over hundreds of years, the Venetians used their skills as sailors to build not only a city, but a huge trading empire.

There are no cars, trucks, or motorcycles in Venice. There is a road that connects the city to the mainland, and a train station. But wheeled transportation stops at the edge of the city. To travel any farther, you need to take a boat, or walk on canal-side paths.

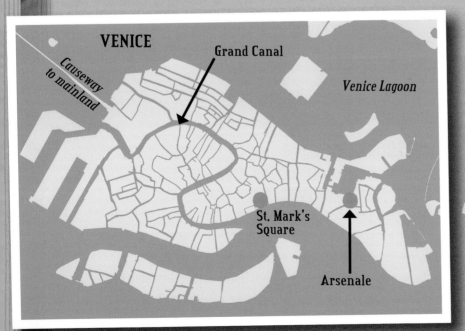

VENICE

Causeway to mainland

Grand Canal

Venice Lagoon

St. Mark's Square

Arsenale

VENICE

ADRIATIC SEA

Water bus on the Grand Canal

MILLIONS OF TOURISTS visit Venice every year. Visitors spending money create many jobs. However, tourism is not without its problems. Huge cruise ships arrive in the summer, and the waves from their engines damage the foundations of buildings in Venice. And with so many wealthy tourists, housing costs are high. Local workers cannot afford to live in Venice.

A PUBLIC WATER BUS, or vaporetto, takes you through the heart of Venice. It sails down the Grand Canal, the city's "Main Street." From the Grand Canal, hundreds of smaller canals branch out just like a network of streets. Alongside the canals are beautiful palaces and churches, as well as shops, hotels, and restaurants.

Your water bus passes St. Mark's Square, the center of government when Venice was still a separate city and not yet part of Italy. For hundreds of years, this stretch of water was Venice's main harbor. Farther along the busy waterfront is the entrance to the Arsenale, the city's ancient naval base. There, warships were built and repaired.

In a city built on water, there are a huge variety of boats. You see police and fire boats, ambulance boats, funeral boats, trash boats, boats full of vegetables, and private water taxis. Most famous are Venice's tourist boats, sleek black gondolas.

Police boat in Venice

Cruise ship and gondola in Venice

PEOPLE ALONG THE WAY

Dani is head waitress at one of Venice's top restaurants. Although she makes a decent amount of money and receives many tips, she cannot afford to live in the city. The only way Dani can have her own apartment is to commute by train from the city of Mestre, on the mainland. There, rent is much cheaper.

Cycle the DANUBE RIVER

EUROPE

GERMANY
CZECH REPUBLIC
SLOVAKIA
MOLDOVA
Passau
Linz   Vienna
Budapest
AUSTRIA
HUNGARY
ROMANIA
Danube Delta
SWITZERLAND
SLOVENIA
CROATIA
BLACK SEA
ITALY
Danube River
BOSNIA AND HERZEGOVINA
SERBIA
BULGARIA
MONTENEGRO   KOSOVO

•••••• Cycle route

The Danube River flows for over 1,700 miles (2,735 km) across central and eastern Europe, from southern Germany to the Black Sea. It has been a key transportation route for centuries, carrying people and goods by boat. Today, people also follow the river on cycle paths.

⬇ **THE DANUBE CYCLE ROUTE** is part of a wider European network of well-maintained cycle paths. Nearly 40,000 cyclists follow it each year. Most choose to ride west to east, from Passau, Germany, across Austria to Vienna, Austria's capital. In this 211-mile (340 km) section, the winds are usually at the riders' backs, making the trip easier. The cycle route avoids major roads, and the scenery is spectacular.

Bicycle riders on the Danube cycle route

Passau, on the Danube River

⬆ **PASSAU,** on the German and Austrian border, is the start of the bicycle journey. This university town of 50,000 was founded where three rivers meet. Tourism is important there, and people come to see the town's historic buildings. Once over the border into Upper Austria, there are forested hills and deep valleys.

Art museum in Vienna, Austria

After passing through Austria's third-largest city, Linz, cyclists enter the Wachau region. This 25-mile (40 km) section of the Danube is famous for its beautiful landscapes. Thousands of people visit every year to see historic castles, wooded hills, and vineyards. The area has warm days and cold nights. This climate helps make the Wachau an important wine-producing area.

PEOPLE ALONG THE WAY

Rudi and Angela are winemakers in the Wachau region. For years, they only sold their wines to local people. With the development of the Danube cycle route, they now take orders from foreign visitors too. As a result their winemaking business has grown.

⬆ **HISTORIC VIENNA** is Austria's capital. It is also the country's largest city, with 1.8 million inhabitants. Its location on the Danube River has provided good transportation links, helping the city to grow. Vienna is famous for its art, music, and culture.

Most cycle trips end at Vienna, but some people follow the river through Hungary to its capital, Budapest. With more than 1.7 million people, Budapest is one of the largest cities on the Danube. From there, the river flows another 1,037 miles (1,670 km) through Croatia, Serbia, Bulgaria, and Romania. Finally, it empties into the Black Sea at the Danube Delta. This is the largest river delta in Europe. It is a wetland area, so few people live there. The delta is known for its birdlife, which includes ducks, pelicans, and herons.

Pelicans in the Danube Delta, Romania

Ferry to the GREEK ISLANDS

Greece is the home of one of the world's great ancient civilizations. In the seas surrounding the country are islands both big and small. Some islands attract huge numbers of tourists every year. Greeks have depended on ships and the sea for thousands of years. Because Greece has a mountainous landscape, travel by boat was the easiest way to move between settlements.

▼ **THE HEART** of Greece's sea **trade** today is Piraeus. This port city is not far from the capital, Athens. It is where we start our ferry journey. In Piraeus's harbor, huge container ships and ferries lie next to the yachts of the super rich. There are also smaller fishing boats. Tourists and Greeks alike line up to board ferries sailing to some of Greece's 227 inhabited islands.

Many Greek islanders traditionally did jobs connected with the sea, such as fishing. Farming, including olive growing and winemaking, was also a way of life. This changed in the 1970s when low-cost air travel began to bring millions of tourists to Greece. Small islands became tourist hot spots as developers created hotels, restaurants, and bars. Greece welcomed 28 million tourists in 2016.

Ferries in the port of Piraeus

NORTH MACEDONIA

BULGARIA

ALBANIA

GREECE

TURKEY

AEGEAN SEA

Athens

Piraeus

Mykonos

Santorini

EUROPE

CRETE

- - - - Ferry route

OUR HIGH-SPEED FERRY, sometimes known as a "Flying Dolphin," takes two hours to reach Mykonos in the Aegean Sea. This popular island can get crowded. The island's regular population of 12,500 increases to more than 50,000 during the summer. Like many Greek islands, Mykonos has to manage its visitors each year. Their huge numbers mean that there is not always enough freshwater for everyone. Tourists also create large amounts of garbage.

Tourists on the beach, Mykonos

FROM MYKONOS, we travel on a slower ferry to Santorini. This beautiful island is located on the remains of a volcano. About 3,500 years ago, it was responsible for one of the biggest **eruptions** in history. This ended human settlement on the island of Santorini for several centuries. Later, new villages developed on the sea cliffs made from the old volcano's crater.

Ferry off Santorini

PEOPLE ALONG THE WAY

Nikos comes from a family of fishers on Santorini. For years the family had little money, but their fortunes changed in the 1970s when Nikos's father began building tourist apartments on the family property. Now Nikos and his brothers own two hotels. Because freshwater supplies are short, they encourage their visitors to save water.

Modern office buildings in Dublin

Fly From IRELAND TO POLAND

The Republic of Ireland, once a poor country, began to get rich when it joined the European Union (EU) in 1973. Today, many EU citizens from other eastern European countries, such as Poland, work in Ireland. These **migrant workers** return home whenever they can. To travel, they take advantage of the low-cost flights now available.

⬆ **DUBLIN,** with a population of more than 1 million, is the largest city in the Republic of Ireland, and the nation's capital. It is also the economic center of Ireland and home to the main European offices of giant global companies such as Microsoft and Amazon.

In the 1800s, millions of people left Ireland because of poverty and poor living conditions. Now, Ireland experiences **immigration** as people travel there to live and work.

Within the European Union, people in one country can freely work in another. When Poland joined the EU in 2004, millions of Poles left home to work in other countries. Jobs in other EU countries are often much better paid than in Poland. This allows workers to save money or send it to their families back home. Dublin is a popular choice as a growing city with plenty of work available.

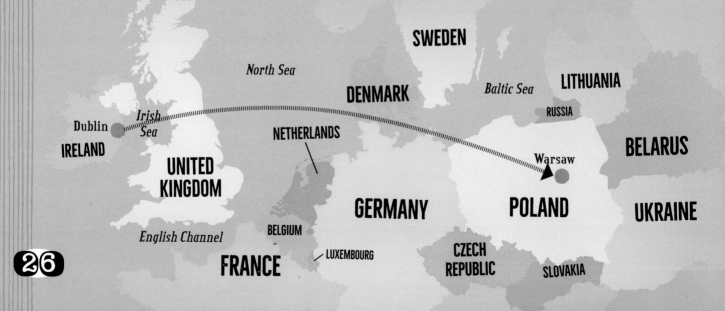

SWEDEN

North Sea

DENMARK

Baltic Sea

LITHUANIA

RUSSIA

Dublin · *Irish Sea*

NETHERLANDS

BELARUS

Warsaw ▶

IRELAND

UNITED KINGDOM

GERMANY

POLAND

UKRAINE

English Channel

BELGIUM

⟋ LUXEMBOURG

CZECH REPUBLIC

SLOVAKIA

FRANCE

Old Town, Warsaw

↓ LOW-COST AIRLINES have changed the face of work and leisure in Europe since the 1990s. Companies such as Ireland's Ryanair and Britain's EasyJet offer frequent, inexpensive flights to European cities. A Polish worker can fly from Dublin to Warsaw in 2 hours and 50 minutes. These short, cheap flights make it easy for people to live and work in different countries.

↑ WARSAW, the capital of Poland, is the biggest city in the country and home to nearly 2 million people. Located on the Vistula River, Warsaw is the political center of Poland, as well as an important business and cultural city. It is home to many new electronics and food companies. Money sent home by Polish workers in other countries has helped Poland become richer. As a result, Warsaw and other cities have improved **infrastructure** such as roads.

Boarding an airplane at Dublin's airport

Pause for
REFLECTION

- How do large numbers of migrant workers impact communities?
- What are the positive and negative effects of low-cost airlines? For example, are the benefits of easy travel more important than the pollution that airplanes cause?

Road --- Ferry

North Sea

WALES

ENGLAND

NETHERLANDS

Amsterdam

Harwich

Hoek van
Holland

Cardiff

GERMANY

M4 highway

London

BELGIUM

FRANCE

EUROPE

Trucking From
AMSTERDAM
TO CARDIFF

An extensive and well-maintained road network helps European manufacturers and farmers to transport their goods to markets quickly. Along major routes, businesses have grown up to take advantage of the opportunities that road transportation offers.

Flowers at Aalsmeer market

⬇ **THE DUTCH FLOWER INDUSTRY** is one example of a business that relies on good road connections. Flower growing and trading is worth millions of dollars per year to the economy of the Netherlands. Every weekday, truckloads of cut flowers leave the flower market at Aalsmeer, about half an hour from the city center of Amsterdam. They drive to customers, such as hotels and flower shops, all over Europe.

The flower market is held in a huge building that covers 5,580,000 square feet (518,000 square m). This is about the size of 97 football fields. Inside the market, **flower traders** sit in front of computer screens and buy thousands of flowers by pressing buttons. Once the traders have bought their flowers, they have to be shipped out as quickly as possible.

New buildings in Cardiff

Highway near London

▲ **JOURNEY'S END IS CARDIFF,** the center of government for Wales. The city has a population of more than 300,000. Many parts of the city have been rebuilt since the 1980s. Cardiff's economy relies on the financial and media industries, among many others.

Like most European countries, the United Kingdom depends on its network of highways. The transportation links and access to markets that highways provide mean that many businesses decide to set up in "corridors" along important road routes. Nearby towns benefit from the trade these roads bring, adding new jobs and bringing in people. The M4 highway corridor is one example. There are negative sides to highways too. High numbers of vehicles result in traffic jams, and noise and air pollution.

▲ **A TYPICAL FLOWER TRUCK** journey might involve a three-day trip to supply customers in the United Kingdom. First, the truck takes the ferry across the North Sea from the port of Hoek van Holland. It arrives at Harwich, on the east coast of the UK. The driver then heads west, delivering flowers in London and along the route of the M4 highway.

PEOPLE
ALONG
THE WAY

Henk runs a company selling Dutch flowers. When the European Union expanded in 2004, new opportunities opened up for him. It meant he could easily travel to and sell flowers in eastern Europe. He now regularly supplies customers in Poland, Hungary, Romania, and elsewhere.

GLOSSARY

canal A human-made waterway with paths on its sides

cargo containers Large metal boxes used to transport goods by ship, rail, and truck

Christian Someone who believes that Jesus Christ was the son of God, and follows his teachings

climate The usual weather conditions of regions over a long period of time

climate change Change in climate patterns around the world due to global warming, or the gradual increase in Earth's temperature

commuters People who regularly travel, usually some distance, to and from work and home

delta A D-shaped area of flat land, often marshy, where a river or rivers empty into a sea or ocean

dikes Walls built to prevent floods

economy The system by which goods and services are made, sold, bought, and used

eruptions For volcanoes, when very hot, liquid rock and gas explode from beneath the ground

fjord A narrow inlet of the sea between high cliffs or hills

flower traders People who buy and sell flowers

foundations Structures that support a building

glaciers Slow-moving masses or rivers of ice

hemisphere One-half of Earth, above or below the equator

herding A way of farming large groups, or herds, of animals, by moving them from one place to another

hostels Low-cost hotels, sometimes run by volunteers or charitable organizations

immigration Coming to live permanently in one country from another

infrastructure The service networks of a country, such as highways, railroads, airports, power plants, and water systems

lagoon A shallow body of water partly enclosed by strips of land or a coral reef

landscape The appearance of a country or area

manufacturing industry Businesses that make things in factories, such as cars or televisions

medieval Referring to the time in history between about 800 and 1500 C.E.

migrant workers People who travel to another country to try to find work

North Pole The northern endpoint of Earth's imaginary axis, around which it spins, located at 90 degrees north

opera A musical entertainment in a theater that tells a story with singers wearing costumes

pedestrians People on foot

pilgrim Someone who makes a long or difficult journey for religious reasons

pilgrimage A journey made by a pilgrim

plateau An area of mainly flat, high ground

port A place where ships load and unload cargo

Roman Empire An empire, centered on the city of Rome, that ruled large parts of Europe around 2,000 years ago

saint A holy person

social housing Inexpensive housing built by cities or governments for people who are less well-off

strait An area of water situated between two large areas of land

suburbs Areas surrounding a city where people live

trade Buying and selling goods and services

United Kingdom A country that includes Great Britain (made up of England, Scotland, and Wales) and Northern Ireland

Further INFORMATION

BOOKS

DK. *People and Places: A Visual Encyclopedia.* DK Children, 2019.

National Geographic Kids. *National Geographic Kids World Atlas.* National Geographic, 2018.

Rockett, Paul. *Mapping Europe.* Crabtree Publishing, 2017.

WEBSITES

www.europa.eu/learning-corner/home_en
Check out games and learning materials about the European Union from the official EU website.

www.kids-world-travel-guide.com/europe-facts.html
This is the Europe section of a website aimed at curious children who dream of traveling.

www.ducksters.com/geography/europe.php
Provides fun facts, geography, and information about Europe, including countries that are not members of the EU.

INDEX

ABOUT THE AUTHOR

John C. Miles studied classical music, history, and English, before working as an editor and writer of children's nonfiction books. Through his work, John has been able to pursue his love of writing about geography, history, and travel.